New People Forever

Experiencing God's Story Series

The Story Begins: The Authority of the Bible, the Triune God, the Great and Good God

The Hero Who Restores: Humanity, Satan and Sin, Jesus Christ

The Rescue: Salvation, the Holy Spirit, the Church

New People Forever: Transformation, Mission, the End

Experiencing God's Story #4

New People Forever

Transformation, Mission, the End

J. Scott Duvall

Kregel
Publications

New People Forever: Transformation, Mission, the End

© 2009 by J. Scott Duvall

Published by Kregel Publications, a division of Kregel, Inc., P.O. Box 2607, Grand Rapids, MI 49501.

This material is also published as part of a workbook under the title *Experiencing God's Story of Life and Hope: A Workbook for Spiritual Formation*, © 2008 and published by Kregel Publications.

ISBN 978-0-8254-2598-1

Printed in the United States of America

09 10 11 12 13 / 5 4 3 2 1

CONTENTS

I would like to thank the following people for their help in developing this resource: Brandon O'Brien, Josh and Jill McCarty, Michael and Terese Cox, Julie (Byrum) Stone, Kristine (Lewis) Smith, and Brandon Holiski. The other pastoral leaders at Fellowship Church—Scott Jackson, Neal Nelson, and Darrell Bridges—have been very encouraging throughout the process. My daughter Meagan spent hours sitting in my office punching holes in each page and compiling the first round of books. Thanks, everyone!

Read Me First

Whether you were raised in the church and accepted Christ as your personal savior at age five, or whether you have only recently given your life to Christ, spiritual growth is not optional. God expects his children to *grow up!*

We define *spiritual formation* as the process of allowing God to conform us to the image of Jesus Christ. The Bible clearly teaches that God wants his children to grow to maturity. As you read the sampling of verses below, especially notice the italicized words.

> For those God foreknew he also predestined to be *conformed to the likeness of his Son*, that he might be the firstborn among many brothers. (Rom. 8:29)

> Therefore, I urge you, brothers, in view of God's mercy, to offer your bodies as living sacrifices, holy and pleasing to God—this is your spiritual act of worship. Do not conform any longer to the pattern of this world, but *be transformed* by the renewing of your mind. Then you will be able to test and approve what God's will is—his good, pleasing and perfect will. (Rom. 12:1–2)

> And we, who with unveiled faces all reflect the Lord's glory, are *being transformed into his likeness* with ever-increasing glory, which comes from the Lord, who is the Spirit. (2 Cor. 3:18)

> Therefore we do not lose heart. Though outwardly we are wasting away, yet inwardly *we are being renewed* day by day. (2 Cor. 4:16)

> My dear children, for whom I am again in the pains of childbirth *until Christ is formed in you* . . . (Gal. 4:19)

> You were taught, with regard to your former way of life, to put off your old self, which is being corrupted by its deceitful desires; to *be made new* in the attitude of your minds; and to put on the new self, *created to be like God* in true righteousness and holiness. (Eph. 4:22–24)

. . . being confident of this, that *he who began a good work in you will carry it on to completion* until the day of Christ Jesus. (Phil. 1:6)

Therefore, my dear friends, as you have always obeyed—not only in my presence, but now much more in my absence—continue to *work out your salvation* with fear and trembling, *for it is God who works in you* to will and to act according to his good purpose. (Phil. 2:12–13)

Have nothing to do with godless myths and old wives' tales; rather, *train yourself to be godly.* (1 Tim. 4:7)

Like newborn babies, crave pure spiritual milk, so that by it *you may grow up in your salvation*, now that you have tasted that the Lord is good. (1 Peter 2:2–3)

Each aspect of our definition of *spiritual formation* is significant. Spiritual formation is a *process*. We don't experience growth as a neat, clean, upward slope toward heaven. In reality it looks and feels more like a roller-coaster ride, twisting and turning and looping and climbing and dropping. Only as you stand back and see the big picture can you tell that the "exit" to the ride is higher than the "entrance." Spiritual formation is a messy process. Because we don't always cooperate with the Lord, it takes time for him to accomplish his purpose in our lives. Philippians 1:6 offers a great deal of encouragement here (see above). God never stops working.

Spiritual formation is the process of *allowing* God to work in our lives. God is sovereign but he has also created us to make important decisions and to bear the responsibility for those decisions. We have no power in and of ourselves to cause our own growth, nor will God force us to obey him. We must allow God to work in our lives and to bring about change. God deeply desires to work, but we must give him the necessary time and space. We don't cause our own growth, but we do cooperate with God as he works. Check out Philippians 2:12–13 above.

Spiritual formation is a process of allowing *God* to work in our lives. We are told that the Holy Spirit continues the earthly ministry that Jesus began (Acts 1:1–2). God's Spirit lives within each genuine believer (1 Cor. 6:19). Our growth is not the result of special circumstances or good luck. We don't grow by our own willpower or by striving to obey the Law. We grow when we follow the Holy Spirit, who alone can produce spiritual fruit in our lives (see Gal. 5:16–23). For us to be loving, joyful, peaceful, and so on, the Holy Spirit must be allowed to do his work.

Spiritual formation is the process of allowing God *to conform us* to the image of Jesus. As much as I hate to admit it, growth means change. Like clay in the potter's hand, we are shaped and molded and conformed to a particular pattern. Change at the hand of God is sometimes painful, but it is always good. We don't always like it, but deep down we always desire it because we know it is necessary. James tells us to "consider it pure joy . . . whenever you face trials of many kinds, because you know that the testing of your faith develops perseverance" and "perseverance must finish its work so that you may be mature and complete, not lacking anything" (James 1:2–4). God loves us too much to let us stay as we are.

Finally, spiritual formation is the process of allowing God to conform us *to the image of Jesus Christ.* In Romans 8:29; 2 Corinthians 3:18; and Galatians 4:19 (see page 9), we are told that God is making us more and more like his Son. Jesus is the perfect pattern or model. He represents the goal of spiritual formation. We are not being shaped into merely religious people or ethical people or church-going people. We are being conformed to the very character of Christ himself.

Everyone, without exception, experiences some kind of "spiritual formation." Dallas Willard puts it this way:

> All people undergo a process of spiritual formation. Their spirit is formed, and with it their whole being. . . . Spiritual formation is not something just for especially religious people. No one escapes. The most hardened criminal as well as the most devout of human beings have had a spiritual formation. They have become a certain kind of person. You have had a spiritual formation and I have had one, and it is still ongoing. It is like education: everyone gets one—a good one or a bad one. (*Renovation of the Heart*, 45)

Everyone is being formed by certain powers after a particular pattern or model. We are blessed beyond words to be able to participate in God's design for spiritual formation.

God often uses resources to shape or mold us into conformity with Christ's character. Of course, the primary resource is God's Word, the Bible. But there are also many good and helpful supplementary resources. We certainly know that no ministry resource of any kind can ever substitute for a personal relationship with God through Jesus Christ, but God does seem to use spiritual-growth resources to help our love for him grow deeper and stronger. The Experiencing God's Story series is one particularly effective resource that God can use to help us understand and participate consistently in true, godly spiritual formation.

Believing-Behaving-Becoming

Most resources focus on just one aspect of the spiritual formation process. Some tools emphasize our *beliefs* by explaining the core teachings of the Christian faith. Knowing what to believe is crucial, but there is more. Many spiritual formation resources highlight how we should *behave.* They stress the importance of spiritual disciplines such as prayer, Bible study, solitude, worship, and so on. Without a doubt God uses such disciplines to transform our lives, but the disciplines are means to an end, not the end themselves.

The disciplines are like workout routines pointing toward the game itself. The game is our life with God. Finally, there are a handful of resources that pay attention to what people are *becoming* in the entire process of spiritual formation (i.e., godly character). Most of these center on the fruit of the Spirit as the true test of spirituality, and rightly so.

The Experiencing God's Story series connects all three aspects of spiritual formation: what we believe, how we behave, and who we are becoming. All three are essential to our growth:

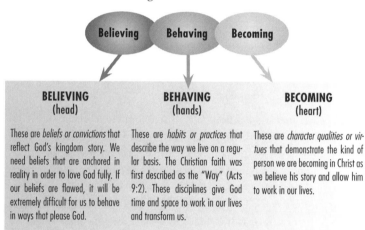

BELIEVING (head)	BEHAVING (hands)	BECOMING (heart)
These are *beliefs or convictions* that reflect God's kingdom story. We need beliefs that are anchored in reality in order to love God fully. If our beliefs are flawed, it will be extremely difficult for us to behave in ways that please God.	These are *habits or practices* that describe the way we live on a regular basis. The Christian faith was first described as the "Way" (Acts 9:2). These disciplines give God time and space to work in our lives and transform us.	These are *character qualities or virtues* that demonstrate the kind of person we are becoming in Christ as we believe his story and allow him to work in our lives.

As a teaching tool, each workbook in this series connects a "Believing" area with a "Behaving" area and a "Becoming" area. Look at the overview on pages 16–17 to see the whole plan. For example, in the third row of the overview you will notice a belief in a great and good God. That belief is connected to the habit of worship and to the quality of purity or holiness. In other words, each row of the overview is connected and integrated; each belief is tied to a behavior or habit and then to a character quality.

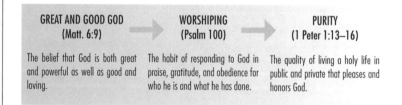

GREAT AND GOOD GOD (Matt. 6:9)	WORSHIPING (Psalm 100)	PURITY (1 Peter 1:13–16)
The belief that God is both great and powerful as well as good and loving.	The habit of responding to God in praise, gratitude, and obedience for who he is and what he has done.	The quality of living a holy life in public and private that pleases and honors God.

This Believing-Behaving-Becoming arrangement is merely a teaching tool and is not intended as a rigid religious system. Sometimes beliefs lead to behavior, while at other times behavior influences beliefs. I'm not suggesting a 1-2-3, neat, clean, foolproof, linear progression that will solve all of life's problems. We all know that life is messy, dynamic, unpredictable, confusing, spontaneous, mystical, and so on. But I still think there are important connections to be made using this teaching arrangement. For instance, what we believe about Satan and sin will affect how we fight spiritual battles and how we understand and experience true freedom. While recognizing this somewhat artificial organization, I hope the Believing-Behaving-Becoming setup encourages you to allow the Lord to work in your entire life rather than just one area of your life.

The four study guides in this series include a total of thirty-six boxes of beliefs, behaviors, and character qualities.

Why these particular topics? Were they chosen simply because they are the most popular topics when it comes to spiritual growth? Are we looking at a random bunch of beliefs and habits and virtues all loosely connected? Actually, the topics were not chosen at random or through some popularity contest. These topics reflect God's story and in our context today we definitely need to stay anchored to God's story.

Experiencing God's Story of Life and Hope

Since the late 1960s we have been experiencing a cultural shift from modernism to postmodernism. (See Jimmy Long's excellent book *Emerging Hope* for more on this cultural change and how Christians can respond.) The modern era emphasized the individual, objective truth, words, and some kind of grand story to explain the meaning of life. By contrast, the postmodern era emphasizes community, subjective "truth," images, and the absence of any grand story to explain life. Christians can embrace some aspects of postmodernism and probably need to resist others. For instance, we can certainly celebrate the greater emphasis on community. But if we give up on a big story that explains reality, then we might as well give up on our faith.

The Christian faith is founded upon God's grand story revealed in the Bible. Postmodernism does away with all big stories that claim to explain reality, opting instead for local or small-group stories. What is true for me and my friends is what is true—period! But Christians can't abandon God's grand story or there is nothing left to believe and all hope is lost. Instead, we need to understand God's story even more and see how it connects to life and how it does us good. We would say that what is real and true is not just what my local group prefers, but what God has revealed. God's story explains life.

Spiritual formation needs to be connected to God's story or it can be manipulated to mean almost anything. In other words, we need a biblical story approach to spiritual formation. But we obviously need to do more than just "believe" the story. We need to act upon the story and allow God's story to shape our whole being. Perhaps now the title makes more sense. We need to experience (beliefs, habits, character qualities) God's story (as revealed in the Bible) of life and hope (a story that does what is best for us).

How is this story approach built into these workbooks? It's simple. If you look again at the overview you will notice that the "Believing" column is actually God's grand story.

BELIEVING	(meaning in the story)
Authority of the Bible	A trustworthy script for the story
Triune God who is Great and Good	Begins with God who is community
Humanity	God wants to share his community
Satan and Sin	Evil powers try to ruin the plan
Jesus Christ	The hero of the story
Salvation	The rescue begins
Holy Spirit	God with us until the end
The Church	The community being rescued
Transformation	God works among his children
Mission	God works through his children
The End	The end—we are with God in the new creation

The very first item in the column is the *Bible* or the script of the story. The story proper begins with *God*—who he is and what he has done. God creates *human beings* to relate to him in perfect community, but *Satan and sin* spoil God's good creation and interfere with his story. God must now attempt a rescue to save his creation. Because of his great love for us, God sent his Son *Jesus Christ* to rescue us from Satan and sin and restore us to a relationship with him. *Salvation* means that God has come to rescue us from the dark side. Through Christ, God offers us a way home. As we respond to his gracious offer by trusting him, we are adopted by God into his family. He puts his very own *Spirit* within us and incorporates us into his community. God desires to use this *new community* (called *church*) to provide us with identity, stability, and wholeness. As we eat, pray, worship, and listen to God's Word together, we begin to feel safe. We open up, revealing our joys and struggles. We discover that we can really be known and loved at the same time, rather than just one or the other. Perhaps for the first time we experience life and hope through Christ and his community. We are *transformed* into the kind of person we were created to be. Naturally, we want other people to experience this life and hope. We have a *mission*—to live out God's story in biblical community so that others can join God's community. Since it is a story of hope, God's story *ends* happily (read Rev. 21:1–4).

To summarize, the "Believing" column is God's grand story. Spiritual formation is anchored in God's story. As we move through the story (from top to bottom), each Belief area extends out (from left to right) to a Behaving and a Becoming area. In this way our whole life is being shaped by the Lord and the entire process is firmly secured to God's story.

Workbook Format

Most of the studies in these workbooks consist of the following elements:

- An introduction that explores the biblical context
- "A Closer Look," to dig deeper into a particular text
- "Crossing the Bridge," to move from the ancient world to our world
- "So What?" to apply what we have discovered in the context of biblical community
- "The Power of Words," to help you understand the meaning of words in the text
- Insightful quotes that inspire reflection and action
- Application questions for your small group
- Cross-references for more Bible exploration
- A "For Deeper Study" recommended reading list

In terms of assumptions, characteristics, and benefits, the Experiencing God's Story series is:

- theologically grounded in the evangelical Christian tradition
- spiritually integrated by connecting believing, behaving, and becoming
- academically reliable through the use of solid biblical scholarship
- pedagogically interactive without being insulting (i.e., you won't find rhetorical fill-in-the-blank questions)
- creatively designed to be used by individuals within the context of biblical community
- practically and realistically arranged into four books, each with 3 three-part chapters

Another subtle characteristic worth mentioning is that the workbooks teach by example how to do responsible Bible study. The move from context to observation to theological principle to application follows the journey model detailed in *Grasping God's Word* by Scott Duvall and Daniel Hays.

May the Lord bless you richly as you allow him to conform you to the image of Jesus Christ. I pray that the Experiencing God's Story series will serve you well on your journey.

Overview of the Experiencing God's Story Series

	BELIEVING	BEHAVING	BECOMING
The Story Begins	**Authority of the Bible** (2 Tim. 3:16–17) The belief that the Bible is God's inspired Word given to us to help us mature in our faith.	**Studying the Bible** (2 Tim. 2:15) The habit of reading, interpreting, and applying the Bible as the primary means of listening to God.	**Truth** (Eph. 4:20–25) The quality of living and speaking truthfully in a world of lies and deception.
	Triune God (Gal. 4:4–6) The belief that the Bible teaches the triune (three-in-one) nature of God.	**Fellowshiping** (Acts 2:42–47) The habit of living in authentic relationship with and dependence upon other followers of Jesus.	**Love** (1 John 4:7–8) The quality of choosing to do what God says is best for another person.
	Great and Good God (Matt. 6:9) The belief that God is both great and powerful as well as good and loving.	**Worshiping** (Psalm 100) The habit of responding to God in praise, gratitude, and obedience for who he is and what he has done.	**Purity** (1 Peter 1:13–16) The quality of living a holy life in public and private that pleases and honors God.
The Hero Who Restores	**Humanity** (Gen. 1:26–28) The belief that human beings are uniquely created in the image of God.	**Seeking the Kingdom** (Matt. 6:33) The habit of acknowledging that God is our Creator and that we are creatures intended to seek him and his purposes.	**Rest** (Matt. 11:28–30) The quality of living with a deep awareness of and contentment with God's purpose for our lives.
	Satan and Sin (Gen. 3:1–7) The belief that Satan is the leader of the opposition against God and his people, and that all human beings have a willful opposition to God's claim on their lives (sin).	**Waging Spiritual War** (Matt. 4:1–11) The habit of knowing and using appropriate strategies for fighting against the Devil, the flesh, and the world.	**Freedom** (Rom. 8:1–4) The quality of experiencing freedom from Satan's power and sin's domination and freedom for new life with God.
	Jesus Christ (John 1:1–3, 14, 18) The belief that Jesus Christ is God the Son, fully divine and fully human.	**Following** (Mark 8:34–38) The habit of daily choosing to follow Jesus Christ as Lord in every area of life.	**New Identity in Christ** (John 21:15–23) The quality of single-minded allegiance to Jesus Christ above every other competing loyalty.

BELIEVING	BEHAVING	BECOMING	
Salvation (Eph. 2:8–10) The belief that salvation is by grace (source), through faith (means), for good works (result).	**Trusting and Acting** (Phil. 2:12–13) The habit of allowing God to work in our lives so that our faith results in action (not salvation by works, but true faith that works).	**Assurance** (Rom. 8:15–16) The quality of knowing (with a healthy confidence) that we belong to God.	The Rescue
Holy Spirit (John 14:16–17) The belief that God the Spirit continues Jesus' earthly ministry, especially that of transforming believers and empowering them to fulfill their mission.	**Walking by the Spirit** (Gal. 5:16, 25) The habit of living in dependence upon the Holy Spirit as the source of strength to resist temptation and imitate Jesus Christ.	**Fruit of the Spirit** (Gal. 5:22–24) The quality of bearing the fruit of the Holy Spirit (Christlike character qualities) in one's life.	
The Church (1 Peter 2:4–10) The belief that God's people are joined together in Christ into a new community, the church.	**Serving** (Mark 10:35–45) The habit of being a servant to other members of this new community.	**Humility** (Luke 18:9–14) The quality of a servant's attitude grounded in the recognition of our status before God and our relationship to others.	
Transformation (Rom. 12:1–2) The belief that we are not to be conformed to this world, but we are to be transformed into the image of Jesus Christ.	**Praying** (Matt. 6:9–13) The habit of continual communion with God that fosters our relationship and allows for genuine transformation in our lives.	**Peace** (Phil. 4:6–7) The quality of calmness and well being (vs. worry and inner turmoil) that comes as a result of our communion with God.	New People Forever
Mission (Matt. 28:18–20) The belief that Jesus commissioned his church to make disciples of all nations.	**Engaging the World** (Acts 1:7–8) The habit of engaging the world for the purpose of sharing the good news of Jesus Christ.	**Compassion** (Luke 10:30–37) The quality of extending love and compassion to people in need.	
The End (1 Thess. 4:13–18) The belief that Jesus Christ will return to judge evil, restore his creation, and live forever in intimate fellowship with his people.	**Persevering** (Heb. 12:1–2) The habit of enduring and persisting in spite of the trials and difficulties we face in life.	**Hope** (Rom. 8:22–25) The quality of a confident expectation that in the end God will be true to his word and keep his promises.	

Trying Versus Training

Transformation

Let's review for a minute. We have said that spiritual formation is the process of allowing the Holy Spirit to conform us to the image of Jesus Christ. God often uses resources such as the Experiencing God's Story series to help the process along. We won't always obey God just because we ought to. We will obey God because in him alone we find life and hope. In our heart of hearts we want to respond to God's gift of life with a deeper and stronger love for him. God desires this kind of whole-life response that connects believing, behaving, and becoming, all of which are rooted and grounded in God's kingdom story as revealed in Scripture (see the Believing columns of the overview, pages 16–17). In Ephesians 3:14–21 Paul prays that his readers might understand and experience God's great story. Read his prayer slowly and pray it for yourself:

> When I think of the wisdom and scope of God's plan, I fall to my knees and pray to the Father, the Creator of everything in heaven and on earth. I pray that from his glorious, unlimited resources he will give you mighty inner strength through his Holy Spirit. And I pray that Christ will be more and more at home in your hearts as you trust in him. May your roots go down deep into the soil of God's marvelous love. And may you have the power to understand, as all God's people should, how wide, how long, how high, and how deep his love really is. May you experience the love of Christ, though it is so great you will never fully understand it. Then you will be filled with the fullness of life and power that comes from God. Now glory be to God! By his mighty power at work within us, he is able to accomplish infinitely more than we would ever dare to ask or hope. May he be given glory in the church and in Christ Jesus forever and ever through endless ages. Amen. (NLT)

When it comes to transformation, artists and athletes have it right. They grasp what the rest of us sometimes miss—that growth is an intentional process. Whether it be voice lessons or choir rehearsal, soccer practice or

"God's mercy"—The underlying Greek term translated "mercy" by the NIV is plural—"mercies." Romans 1–11 spells out the many ways that God has poured out his mercies on us. The command to "offer" our bodies to God is based upon these mercies. We don't obey in order to earn mercy; rather, God's mercy is the basis for our obedience—the only appropriate response to God's grace (cf. Rom. 6:13, 16, 19).

"living sacrifices, holy and pleasing"—The sacrifices we offer to God are described in three ways: living, holy, and pleasing to God. Unlike sacrificial animals that were put to death, we go on living. As sacrifices, our lives should be set apart and pleasing to God. This is true worship.

"spiritual act of worship"—Offering ourselves as sacrifices to God is equated with "spiritual worship." The adjective translated "spiritual" (*logikos*) probably refers to the idea of "informed" or "deliberate." Again, unlike sacrificial animals that did not understand what was happening to them, we give ourselves to God willingly and with full understanding. The word "worship" (KJV: "service") should be understood broadly to include all of life and not just a time of praise.

volleyball drills, artists and athletes understand that growth takes time and effort. They are not just trying harder; they have entered a life of training. John Ortberg describes the difference between *trying* and *training*:

> For much of my life, when I heard messages about following Jesus, I thought in terms of *trying hard* to be like him. So after hearing . . . a sermon on patience on Sunday, I would wake up on Monday morning determined to be a more patient person. Have you ever tried hard to be patient with a three-year-old? I have—and it generally didn't work any better than would my trying hard to run a marathon for which I had not trained. I would end up exhausted and defeated. . . . . Spiritual transformation is not a matter of trying harder, but of training wisely. (*Life You've Always Wanted*, 47)

What would you say are some differences between trying and training?

A Closer Look—Romans 12:1–2

One of the key texts on transformation is found at the beginning of Romans 12. Our focal passage serves as the bridge between the more "theological" section of Romans 1–11 and the more "practical" section of Romans 12–16 (see "Make It Practical" on page 22). Take time to dig deep into God's Word. Circle the verbs, put a box around the key nouns, and note the lists and what they describe. Identify the contrasts, the conjunctions, the explanations of how and why, along with result statements. Read "The Power of Words" to the left. Don't miss a thing. This is one juicy passage!

[1]Therefore, I urge you, brothers [and sisters], in view of God's mercy, to offer your bodies as living sacrifices, holy and pleasing to God—this is your spiritual act of worship. [2]Do not conform any longer to the pattern of this world, but be transformed by the renewing of your mind. Then you will be able to test and approve what God's will is—his good, pleasing and perfect will.

Crossing the Bridge

Remember, a theological principle is a present-tense statement of a timeless truth that applies equally well to the biblical audience and to us. What theological principles do you see in Romans 12:1–2?

- Our worship is a response to God's mercy. Mercy always comes before obedience.

- Worship includes offering both the body and the mind to God. The Christian life is not just a mental game. If we do not offer our bodies, we do not worship.

-

-

-

Spiritual Disciplines

Transformation takes time and effort. I am not suggesting that we can earn salvation by good works but encouraging us to admit that a genuine experience of grace produces fruit. Sometimes we use grace as an excuse *not* to offer our bodies or to resist conformity to the world or to renew our minds, unless we are put "on the spot" to be like Jesus. Dallas Willard illustrates what usually happens when we try to act like Christ only when we are put to the test:

> Think of certain young people who idolize an outstanding baseball player. . . . When they are playing in a baseball game, they all try to behave exactly as their favorite baseball star does. . . . These young people try anything and everything their idol does, hoping to be like him—they buy the type of shoes the star wears, the same glove he uses, the same bat. . . . Will they succeed in performing like the star, though? . . . We know that they won't succeed if all they do is try to be like him in the game . . . and we all understand why. The star performer himself didn't achieve his excellence by trying to behave in a certain way *only during the game.* Instead, he chose an overall life preparation of mind and body, pouring all his energies into that total preparation, to provide a foundation in the body's automatic responses and strength for his conscious efforts during the game. . . . A baseball player who expects to excel in the game without adequate exercise of his body is no more ridiculous than the Christian who hopes to be able to act in the manner of Christ when put to the test without the appropriate exercise in godly living. . . . We cannot behave "on the spot" as he [Christ] did and

"conform . . . to the pattern of this world"—To be conformed is to be forced into a mold or pattern (cf. 1 Peter 1:14, which we studied in *The Story Begins,* Becoming 3). This "world" (literally, "age") refers to the ungodly mind-set and behavior of those who do not know God (cf. Eph. 2:1–3). The present-tense command suggests that we need to repeatedly refuse to let this "age" mold or shape us.

"be transformed"—The negative command not to conform is replaced with the positive command to be transformed. This word is used to describe Jesus' transfiguration (Matt. 17:2; Mark 9:2) and here refers to the ongoing renewal and change that Jesus brings through his Spirit (see 2 Cor. 3:7–18).

A Transformed Person

A disciplined [or mature] person is someone who can do the right *thing* at the right *time* in the right *way* with the right spirit [or *motive*].

—John Ortberg,
Life You've Always Wanted, 54

Do you need to make an important decision or evaluate a recent action? Use these four questions to evaluate your decision:

- Is this the right thing to do?
- Is the timing right?
- Am I doing this in the right way?
- Am I doing this for the right reason?

taught if in the rest of our time we live as everybody else does. . . . Our efforts to take control *at that moment* will fail so uniformly and so ingloriously that the whole project of following Christ will appear ridiculous to the watching world. (*Spirit of the Disciplines*, 3–7)

We need to enter a life of training and discipline, much like an athlete or an artist. We need to do more than try hard when the pressure is on; we need to train ourselves to be godly as a way of life (1 Tim. 4:7–8). *Spiritual disciplines* are habits or practices that place us before God so that he can transform us. They are tools in God's hands that he uses to shape and mold us to be more like Jesus. Spiritual disciplines include prayer, submission, study, meditation, service, confession, solitude, and silence, just to name a few. Almost any activity can become a training exercise. Spiritual disciplines take us beyond merely trying harder; they enable us to train wisely.

So What?

1. If we are convinced that consistent training is more valuable to spiritual transformation than sporadic trying, why do we so often settle for trying?

2. Both the "body" and the "mind" are mentioned in Romans 12:1–2. Do we associate spiritual growth more with the mind or the body? What do we lose if we neglect the other aspect?

3. As you think about John Ortberg's definition of "A Transformed Person" given on page 21, which one of the four questions do you struggle with the most?

4. Which spiritual discipline has God used to grow you?

5. As you think about Romans 12:1–2, trying versus training, and spiritual disciplines, what specific step do you believe God wants you to take to "test and approve" his good, pleasing, and perfect will?

Cross-References

John 15:4–8; Rom. 6:12–14; 8:29; 1 Cor. 10:31; 2 Cor. 3:7–18; 4:16; Gal. 2:20; 4:19; Eph. 4:22–24; Phil. 1:6; 2:12–13; 3:7–14; Col. 3:10; 1 Tim. 4:7; James 1:2–4; 1 Peter 2:2–3

For Deeper Study

Cloud, Henry, and John Townsend. *How People Grow.* Grand Rapids: Zondervan, 2001.

Moo, Douglas J. *Romans.* NIV Application Commentary. Grand Rapids: Zondervan, 2000.

Willard, Dallas. *Renovation of the Heart.* Colorado Springs: NavPress, 2002.

Willard, Dallas. *The Spirit of the Disciplines.* San Francisco: HarperSanFrancisco, 1988.

Only One Thing Matters

Praying

God's mercy draws us to worship him. True worship occurs when we offer ourselves, bodies and all, to God. Rather than being shaped by ways of the world, we are transformed by God himself. When it comes to transformation, artists and athletes correctly realize that change occurs not just by trying harder in certain on-the-spot situations, but by training consistently over time. Training involves spiritual disciplines or practices that place us before God so that he has time and space to do his transforming work. Prayer is one such spiritual discipline, and many people consider prayer to be the central discipline because it lies at the heart of our relationship with God. Referring to Jesus' statement to a busy and worried woman in Luke 10:42, Henri Nouwen writes, "Prayer is the center of the Christian life. *It is the only necessary thing.* . . . It is living with God here and now" (*Only Necessary Thing*, 25). Prayer is more than just talking to God; prayer is communion with God that comes out of a heart that has experienced the love of God. In Behaving 1 we turn our attention to what Jesus taught his first disciples about communing with the Father.

About 1490 two young friends, Albrecht Dürer and Franz Knigstein, were struggling young artists. Since both were poor, they worked to support themselves while they studied art. Work took so much of their time and advancement was slow. Finally, they reached an agreement: they would draw lots, and one of them would work to support both of them while the other would study art. Albrecht won and began to study, while Franz worked at hard labor to support them. They agreed that when Albrecht was successful he would support Franz who would then study art.

Albrecht went off to the cities of Europe to study. As the world now knows, he had not only talent but genius. When he had attained success, he went back to keep his bargain with Franz. But Albrecht soon discovered the enormous price his friend had paid. For as Franz worked at hard manual labor to support his friend, his fingers had become stiff and twisted. His slender, sensitive hands had been ruined for life. He could no longer execute the delicate brush strokes necessary to fine painting. Though his artistic dreams could never be fully realized, he was not embittered but rather rejoiced in his friend's success.

One day Dürer came upon his friend unexpectedly and found him kneeling with his gnarled hands intertwined in prayer, quietly praying for the success of his friend although he himself could no longer be an artist. Albrecht Dürer, the great genius, hurriedly sketched the folded hands of his faithful friend and later completed a truly great masterpiece known as "The Praying Hands." (Gray, *Stories for the Heart*, 261)

"One day Jesus was praying in a certain place. When he finished, one of his disciples said to him, 'Lord, teach us to pray'" (Luke 11:1). His response has traditionally been called "The Lord's Prayer," although Jesus himself intended it as a model prayer for his followers.

A Closer Look—Matthew 6:9–13

1. Before teaching the disciples how to pray, Jesus teaches them how *not* to pray. Read Matthew 6:5–8 and complete the following chart on what to avoid in prayer.

	"Do not be like the hypocrites" (Matt. 6:5–6)	"Do not keep on babbling like pagans" (Matt. 6:7–8)
Why should we not pray in this way?		
What is the result of praying in this way?		

chart continued on next page...

THE POWER OF WORDS

"**hallowed**"—Since there is no contemporary verb for "holy" in English, we use this older word (we could start using the word *holified*). God is holy and defines what it means to be holy. People and things are holy when they are closely related to God. We are not praying here that God will become holy but that we would treat God as holy.

"**kingdom**"—This term refers to God's rule or reign. The kingdom of God has broken into this world with the coming of Christ and will one day be made known fully at the second coming of Christ. To pray for God's kingdom to come is to (1) pray that more people would come under God's rule now and (2) that God would soon finish the project (e.g., Rev. 22:20).

"**daily bread**"—Most people in Jesus' day were paid at the end of each day. As a result, this is a prayer for God to meet our basic needs, including physical needs, one day at a time. This is a request for needs, not wants. Also, the word "today" reminds us that the present day, rather than the future, should be our focus. God wants us to depend on him continually for our needs.

	"Do not be like the hypocrites" (Matt. 6:5–6)	"Do not keep on babbling like pagans" (Matt. 6:7–8)
How should we pray instead?		

Look at the prayer from Matthew 6:9–13. Looking especially at the pronouns, identify the pattern or organization to the prayer.

[9]Our Father in heaven,

hallowed be your name,

[10]your kingdom come,

your will be done

on earth as it is in heaven.

[11]Give us today our daily bread.

[12]Forgive us our debts, as we also have forgiven our

debtors.

[13]And lead us not into temptation, but deliver us from

the evil one.

THE POWER OF WORDS

"temptation"—This word can be used to refer to a temptation to sin or to a trial or test. Since God does not tempt people to do evil or sin (James 1:13), this is probably a request for God not to lead us into a trial that will be too strong for us and surely result in a fall. This is the idea in Mark 14:38 and Galatians 6:1. In other words, we are praying for spiritual protection.

2. Did you notice that the first three requests are God centered? Write a short paragraph about what you think this part of the prayer means (i.e., God's name, kingdom, and will).

BEHAVING 1—*Praying*

3. The second set of three requests is centered on human beings. One of these requests deals with forgiveness. Read Matthew 6:12, 14–15. What do these verses teach about forgiveness?

Crossing the Bridge

What theological principles do you see in Matthew 6:9–13?

-

-

-

-

Now that you have briefly studied The Lord's Prayer, write a paraphrase of the prayer (i.e., rephrase the prayer in your own words). Make it personal by imagining that Jesus himself is instructing you today about how to pray.

So What?

1. What part of Jesus' teachings on prayer in Matthew 6 do you most need to apply to your life right now?

2. What keeps you from praying more?

What Do You Think?

What do you think C. S. Lewis meant when he said that in prayer "we must lay before Him what is in us, not what ought to be in us" (*Letters to Malcolm*, 22)?

?

Cross-References

1 Sam. 12:23; 2 Chron. 7:14; Neh. 1:4–11; Ps. 143:1; Isa. 56:7; Dan. 6:10; Jonah 2:1–9; Matt. 6:5–15; Mark 1:35; 14:32–39; Luke 5:16; 11:1; John 17; Acts 1:14; 2:42; 13:3; 16:25; Rom. 8:26; Eph. 3:14–21; Phil. 1:3–4; Col. 4:2; 1 Thess. 5:17; James 5:13–16; 1 Peter 3:12; 4:7

For Deeper Study

Foster, Richard J. *Prayer: Finding the Heart's True Home*. San Francisco: HarperSanFrancisco, 1992.

Hybels, Bill. *Too Busy Not to Pray*. Rev. and exp. Downers Grove, IL: InterVarsity Press, 1998.

Lewis, C. S. *Letters to Malcolm Chiefly on Prayer*. New York: Harcourt, 1964.

Nouwen, Henri J. M. *The Only Necessary Thing*. New York: Crossroad, 1999.

Yancey, Philip. *Prayer: Does It Make Any Difference?* Grand Rapids: Zondervan, 2006.

3. What has helped you to stay consistent when it comes to prayer?

4. Read "Prayer Paralysis?" in the sidebar on page 27. Are you paralyzed by thinking that you have to get your life straightened out before you can pray? How can you begin to pray "what is in you," not what ought to be in you?

5. How has God changed you through prayer? Give some examples.

Practicing His Presence

Peace

Our heavenly Father has determined to make us more like the Son. To accomplish his transforming work, the Father often encourages spiritual practices such as prayer. In prayer we open our hearts to God so that he may give us life and hope. Prayer involves a transfer of trust from ourselves—our abilities, our resources, our knowledge, our possessions—to God. Instead of wallowing in worry and fear, we let God know what we are thinking and feeling. As we pray, we begin to change. Sometimes gradually and at other times quickly, the chaos and turmoil and confusion give way to God's peace, a peace that is too wonderful to comprehend fully and too magnificent to achieve. In Becoming 1 we will look at how God's peace comes as the fruit of transformation and prayer.

There is always something to worry about. During the week I was writing this study on peace, I discovered that someone had stolen our credit card and charged over $1,000. Would we lose the money, or would the bank reimburse us? My wife Judy had recently traveled to Louisiana with a group of students to help with disaster relief. She returned with an extremely bad case of poison ivy. Even with all the medication, the itching was painful and caused her to lose sleep. Would this stuff ever go away? During a recent fall break, one of our students had been killed in a car wreck. I did not know the student, but what could I say to those who knew him well? Recently a "friend" made some choices that were both professionally inappropriate and personally disrespectful to me. How should I respond to this situation? Sometimes when it rains, it pours. What is on your worry list?

Although we will always have opportunities to worry, God promises peace when we abide in him through prayer. Have you ever deliberately practiced God's presence by consciously thinking about him throughout the day?

Prayer with Thanksgiving Produces Peace

Matthew Henry is a well-known Bible commentator. One day he was robbed and that evening made the following entry in his diary:

Let me be thankful—first, because I was never robbed before; second, because although they took my wallet they did not take my life; third, because although they took my all, it was not much; and fourth, because it was I who was robbed, not I who robbed.

—Alice Gray,
Stories for the Heart, 86

Frank Laubach (1884–1970), a missionary to the Philippines, knew what it meant to pray without ceasing.

> As I analyze myself I find several things happening to me as a result of these two months of strenuous effort to keep the Lord in mind every minute. This concentration upon God is strenuous, *but everything else has ceased to be so.* I think more clearly, I forget less frequently. Things which I did with a strain before, I now do easily and with no effort whatever. I worry about nothing, and lose no sleep. I walk on air a good part of the time. Even the mirror reveals a new light in my eyes and face. I no longer feel in a hurry about anything. . . . Each minute I meet calmly as though it were not important. Nothing can go wrong excepting one thing. That is that God may slip from my mind if I do not keep on my guard. If He is there, the universe is with me. My task is simple and clear. (Laubach, *Letters*, May 24, 1930)

Whether or not you subscribe to Laubach's approach, one thing is obvious—if we prayed more, we would worry less and experience more of God's peace. Let's go the Scriptures.

A Closer Look—Philippians 4:6–7

In the passage below locate any commands, contrasts, results, promises, figures of speech, descriptions ("which"), and locations ("in").

SCRIPTURE NOTES

> [6]Do not be anxious about anything, but in everything, by prayer and petition, with thanksgiving, present your requests to God.
>
> [7]And the peace of God, which transcends all understanding, will guard your hearts and your minds in Christ Jesus.

A Blessing of Peace

The LORD bless you and keep you; the LORD make his face shine upon you and be gracious to you; the LORD turn his face toward you and give you peace.

—Numbers 6:24–26

1. What do the words "anything" and "everything" indicate?

2. Identify the different words for prayer used in this passage.

3. What attitude should accompany our prayers? Why is this attitude important?

4. What is the major contrast in verse 6?

5. What is the promise contained in verse 7?

6. What kind of work does the "peace of God" do in our lives?

7. Read Philippians 4:1–9. How does the surrounding context help you understand 4:6–7?

Crossing the Bridge

What timeless truths do you see in Philippians 4:6–7?

•

•

•

As you looked closely at Philippians 4:6–7, did you notice that God's peace comes when we pray, not when we get a certain answer to prayer? Long before we get the answer we want or even before we get an answer at all, peace comes through the very act of praying. In prayer we transfer our trust from ourselves and our ability to control life to God and his resources.

As we cast our cares on him, worries are replaced with a calmness of heart and mind. We are *either* worrying *or* praying; never both at the same time. In Matthew 6:25–33, Jesus puts it all in perspective by saying something like, "If you want to worry, worry about something important. Stop stressing over the little stuff like clothes and money, and seek God's kingdom and his righteousness."

So What?

1. From your closer look at Philippians 4:6–7, what is most encouraging and helpful to you?

2. What are the top five things you could be worried about right now in your life?

3. How does praying "with thanksgiving" change your outlook and perspective about the situation you are praying about?

4. If prayer leads to peace and we are not experiencing peace, what do we need to change about the way we pray?

Now it's time to stop answering discussion questions and actually pray about what is making you anxious, fearful, angry, or frustrated. Don't just think about these things; really pray about them.

Cross-References
Num. 6:24–26; Pss. 1:1–3; 23:1–6; 34:14; 46:1–11; 119:165; Prov. 14:30; Isa. 26:3; 41:10; Matt. 6:25–34; 11:28; John 14:27; 16:33; Rom. 8:6; 14:17; 15:13; Gal. 5:22; Phil. 4:8–13; Col. 3:15

For Deeper Study
Baillie, John. *The Diary of Private Prayer*. New York: Scribner, 1949.
Brother Lawrence. *The Practice of the Presence of God*. Reprint. New Kensington, PA: Whitaker House, 1982.
Fee, Gordon D. *Paul's Letter to the Philippians*. New International Commentary on the New Testament. Grand Rapids: Eerdmans, 1995.
Laubach, Frank. *Letters by a Modern Mystic*. Westwood, NJ: Revell, 1958.

Why Are We Still Here?

Mission

Have you ever wondered why God doesn't take us to heaven immediately after we become followers of Jesus Christ? Why does he allow us to stay in this world where Satan prowls around like a lion looking for someone to devour (1 Peter 5:8)? God's kingdom story helps us answer that question.

Triune God · Human Beings · Satan and Sin · Jesus Christ · Holy Spirit · God's People · Spiritual Growth · The Mission · The End

God leaves us on earth even after we have been rescued because he is a missionary God and he wants us to join him in the mission. God has granted us the privilege of living and sharing his kingdom story. We endure the attacks of Satan, the pitfalls of sin, and the many dangers of a fallen world because there are people who need to be rescued.

Think about it this way. Let's suppose that your family lives in an area that is vulnerable to flash flooding. On one occasion torrential rains cause a sudden flood. You are pulled to safety, but in the confusion you mistakenly think that your entire family also has been rescued. Later you realize that your daughter is still trapped in the backyard tree house. You're safe, but someone you deeply love remains in danger. Wouldn't you do everything in your power to bring about a rescue? You bet your life you would!

When it comes to rescuing people from Satan and sin and death, the passion to save comes straight from God's own heart.

> The call of God is to share in his own mission in the world. First, he sent his Son. Then he sent his Spirit. Now he sends his church, that is, us. He sends us out by his Spirit into his world to announce his Son's salvation. He worked through his Son to achieve it; he works through us to make it known. (Stott, *Authentic Christianity*, 316)

After Jesus had been put to death on the cross and raised from the dead, he met with his followers to give them instructions about what to do after he ascended to the Father. Here is what he told them:

All authority in heaven and on earth has been given to me. Therefore go and make disciples of all nations, baptizing them in the name of the Father and of the Son and of the Holy Spirit, and teaching them to obey everything I have commanded you. And surely I am with you always, to the very end of the age. (Matt. 28:18–20)

This is what is written: The Christ will suffer and rise from the dead on the third day, and repentance and forgiveness of sins will be preached in his name to all nations, beginning at Jerusalem. You are witnesses of these things. (Luke 24:46–48)

Peace be with you! As the Father has sent me, I am sending you. (John 20:21)

It's hard to believe that Jesus entrusted the entire mission to such a common, ordinary bunch of people, but the fact is these "average Joes" radically changed their world. They were completely convinced that God's great story had reached its climax in Jesus, the Rescuer or Savior. They believed that God himself had become a man in order to save them from their sins. They weren't just trying to live by a higher law or advocating a new religion. They had found life in the person of Jesus Christ, risen from the dead! How can you keep quiet when you find life? When you know the answer, how can you keep it a secret? You cannot remain silent and passive and apathetic when you experience grace and forgiveness, freedom and hope. When you know what it means to be fully known and fully loved by your Creator, it leads you to worship. We talk about whatever or whomever we worship. We want others to find life and bow down beside us as we worship the Life Giver, to whom be the glory forever and ever. That's our mission.

A Closer Look—Matthew 28:18–20

Our focal passage is part of Jesus' Great Commission to his followers. Here Jesus gives us our mission in this world. Take time to understand what this passage says and means. Circle the repeated words. Underline the pronouns. Double underline the commands. Locate the important conjunctions (e.g., "therefore"). Identify the words or phrases that show means (i.e., how we do something), place, and time. Are there any lists? Do you see any promises? What is God's role? What is our role?

"make disciples"—This command lies at the heart of the Great Commission. A disciple is a committed follower of a teacher or leader (recall our study in *The Hero Who Restores*, Behaving 3). To "make" disciples involves (1) inviting people to begin a relationship with Jesus Christ and (2) helping them grow in that relationship. The command applies not just to the original hearers, but to all disciples. Otherwise his promise at the end of verse 20 would not make much sense.

"nations"—Although the word can refer to all nations except Israel, most scholars think the term refers to all peoples, including Israel. The full phrase "all nations" is used in Matthew 24:9, 14; 25:32 to refer to all peoples (cf. John 3:16). Matthew's gospel begins with Abraham (Matt. 1:1), through whom God promised to bless all peoples, and ends by showing that the promise will be fulfilled through Jesus and his missionary people.

"teaching them to obey"—Evangelism alone does not fulfill the Great Commission. New believers must enter a lifelong process of learning to obey Jesus' teachings. In Jesus' culture only privileged men had access to the leading rabbis. Jesus, however, invites *all* people to follow him. Teaching lies at the heart of the growth process, but this kind of teaching is much more than an academic exercise. Jesus does not say "teaching them to know," but rather "teaching them to obey." Discipleship is education that results in obedience (Matt. 12:49–50).

SCRIPTURE NOTES

¹⁸Then Jesus came to them and said, "All authority in heaven

and on earth has been given to me. ¹⁹Therefore go and make

disciples of all nations, baptizing them in the name of the

Father and of the Son and of the Holy Spirit, [20]and teaching them to obey everything I have commanded you. And surely I am with you always, to the very end of the age."

The structure or organization of the Great Commission is very important. Look at each item below and the role that it plays in the commission. Then in the space after each item, answer the question, What difference does this make? In other words, what difference does it make that the foundation of the commands is the authority of Jesus? What difference does it make that "go" is as much a command as "make disciples"? And so forth.

- Foundation of the commands—"all authority . . . has been given to [Jesus]"

- Supporting command—"go"

- Main command—"make disciples of all nations"

- Explanation of how to carry out the commands (means)—"baptizing" and "teaching"

- Promise for those who carry out the commands—"I am with you always"

Crossing the Bridge

What theological principles do you see in Matthew 28:18–20?

-

-

-

Fuel and Goal of Missions

Missions is not the ultimate goal of the church. Worship is. Missions exists because worship doesn't. Worship is ultimate, not missions, because God is ultimate, not man. When this age is over, and the countless millions of the redeemed fall on their faces before the throne of God, missions will be no more. It is a temporary necessity. But worship abides forever.

Worship, therefore, is the fuel and goal of missions. It's the goal of missions because in missions we simply aim to bring the nations into the white-hot enjoyment of God's glory. . . .

But worship is also the fuel of missions. Passion for God in worship precedes the offer of God in preaching. You can't commend what you don't cherish. . . .

Where passion for God is weak, zeal for missions will be weak.

—John Piper,
Let the Nations Be Glad, 17–18

So What?

1. What do you think Jesus' commission teaches us about how we should use terms such as *disciple* and *discipleship* today?

2. Does your Christian community put more emphasis on beginning the Christian faith (baptizing) or maturing in the faith (teaching)? If the emphasis is out of balance, how could it be adjusted?

3. What motivates you to be more involved in God's mission to rescue lost and hurting people? Try to be honest and specific.

4. What kind of teaching-learning are you experiencing on a weekly basis (e.g., sermons, Bible studies, small groups, personal study, books)?

5. What could make your teaching-learning experiences more focused on learning to obey rather than just learning to know?

6. The commission is to make disciples of all nations or peoples. What are you and your Christian community doing to reach out to people groups around your "world" and around the world?

Disciples = Christians

Everyone who has heard the gospel message and has responded by believing on Jesus for eternal life is a disciple/Christian/believer, all of which are virtually synonymous terms (cf. Acts 2:44; 4:32; 5:14; 6:1, 7; 11:26; 26:28).

Today many incorrectly use the title "disciple" to refer to a person who is more committed than other Christians or to those involved in special "discipleship programs." But we can see from Jesus' commission that all Christians are disciples. It is just that some are obedient disciples, while others are not.

—Michael Wilkins, *Matthew*, 956

Cross-References

Luke 24:45–49; John 17:18; 20:21–23; Acts 1:8; Rom. 10:14–15; 2 Cor. 5:11–20; 1 John 1:2–3

For Deeper Study

Piper, John. *Let the Nations Be Glad: The Supremacy of God in Missions.* 2nd ed. Rev. and exp. Grand Rapids: Baker, 2003.

Wilkins, Michael J. *Following the Master: A Biblical Theology of Discipleship.* Grand Rapids: Zondervan, 1992.

Wilkins, Michael J. *Matthew.* NIV Application Commentary. Grand Rapids: Zondervan, 2004.

Willard, Dallas. *The Great Omission: Reclaiming Jesus' Essential Teachings on Discipleship.* San Francisco: Harper Collins, 2006.

As the Father Has Sent Me, I Am Sending You

Engaging the World

God wants us to join him in his mission of rescuing people from the grip of Satan and sin. That's one reason why we are still on this earth. When Jesus appeared to his followers after his death and resurrection, he said, "Peace be with you! As the Father has sent me, I am sending you" (John 20:21). Our mission is clear—go and make disciples of all nations. But it will remain "mission impossible" unless we rely on the power of the Holy Spirit. God doesn't just give us a job to do and wish us good luck. The Holy Spirit empowers us to do the job of engaging the world with the good news of Jesus. Mark Tabb rightly concludes that "we cannot hide from our culture and change it at the same time" (*Mission to Oz*, 128). In Behaving 2 we will explore ways of living out our mission in this world.

Michael Green, senior research professor at Wycliffe Hall, Oxford University, has conducted a comprehensive study of how the early church lived out the Christian mission. At the beginning of his book titled *Evangelism in the Early Church*, he says that while it was the early church's conviction, passion, and determination that mattered most, they used at least five mission strategies, or methods, that could also prove useful for us (pages 23–27):

1. They did most of their evangelism on secular ground. Wherever they went, they talked about Jesus to anyone who would listen.
2. The early Christians made a priority of personal conversations with individuals. Jesus models this kind of face-to-face approach in his conversation with the woman at the well in John 4.

3. The home provided the most natural context for spreading the gospel. People gathered for food, companionship, learning, and worship in a non-threatening but intentional setting.

4. Church planting proved extremely effective. Green writes, "The leadership was always plural. . . . They were a leadership team. These new churches nearly always begin in a home, soon pack that out, and then hire a hall to meet in. Buildings come along later if at all" (page 25).

5. The first Christians emphasized the work of the Holy Spirit, who transformed their character and gifted them for ministry. Green concludes: "The Western Church has grown too dependent on words, and not nearly dependent enough on the power of the Holy Spirit. . . . Instead of being a community demonstrating the Lord's power, we have become one which talks incessantly" (v. 26). Yet the "kingdom of God is not a matter of talk but of power" (1 Cor. 4:20).

If you believe in engaging the world with the gospel of Jesus Christ but find yourself frustrated, guilt-ridden, or paralyzed when it comes to actually doing so, pray that God would use this teaching and your community group discussion to renew your perspective and passion for carrying out his mission in this world.

A Closer Look—Acts 1:7–8

In our focal passage, look for contrasts, time and place indicators, repeated pronouns, lists, cause-effect relationships, God's responsibility, and our responsibility.

⁷He said to them: "It is not for you to know the times or dates the Father has set by his own authority. ⁸But you will receive power when the Holy Spirit comes on you; and you will be my witnesses in Jerusalem, and in all Judea and Samaria, and to the ends of the earth."

Crossing the Bridge

How does our situation differ from that of the disciples who first heard Jesus speak these words?

What theological principles do you see in Acts 1:7–8?

-
-
-

A Comprehensive Strategy for Engaging the World

How can a Christian community today effectively engage the world with the good news of Jesus Christ? The strategy below is more than just another evangelistic program. Rather, it offers a comprehensive and realistic way of carrying out Jesus' mission in this world. We should always remember that apart from the empowering of God's Spirit, no plan will work.

1. We need to be attentive to how we *live the gospel* ourselves. People today are weary of words. They want to see a changed life before they will listen to any explanation of what caused the change. The integrity of the messenger authenticates the reality of the message.

2. We need to *know God's kingdom story* well enough to be able to converse about the whole story regardless of where our conversation begins. This calls for improving our biblical literacy and our theological understanding of the Christian message. (The kingdom story is summarized in the Believing columns of the overview, pages 16–17).

3. We need to be *connected to a Christian community* that embodies the life and teachings of Jesus. Again, people today are moved to faith as they observe and connect with a community where the kingdom story is fleshed out for all to see. (Read the sidebar quote on page 41 about how the early church did this.)

4. We need to pray that God's Spirit would cultivate in us a *compassion for people*. We should be sensitive to many things in others' lives—change, pain, discontentment, frustration, openness, and so on.

5. We need to *spend time with people who do not have a relationship with Jesus*. This social connection is probably the number one challenge

for most Christians, many of whom simply don't spend any time with non-Christians.

6. We need to engage non-Christians in *honest, authentic conversations* about God and Christ. Many Christians who are equipped to spout off a three-minute, canned gospel presentation have very little aptitude for a more in-depth conversation that centers around the kingdom story. Perhaps the greatest deterrent to these kinds of conversations is fear; yet as Mark Tabb says, "If the gospel is true, it has nothing to fear from conversations with those who don't believe it" (*Mission to Oz*, 114). We must be equipped to listen effectively and to ask questions that will help us understand, not only people's life experiences, but also the story they are counting on to make sense of life.

7. We need to embody the kingdom story through genuinely spiritual responses (fruit of the Spirit in Galatians 5) and *authentic acts of service*. We should not serve for any payoff or personal profit but simply as an expression of God's love.

8. We need to *be the relational bridge* between our non-Christian friends and our Christian community. Today people will often make a commitment to a community where Jesus Christ can be experienced before they will make an individual commitment to Christ. Our relationship serves as the bridge between the church and the world.

9. We need to encourage our friends to make a *personal commitment to Jesus*. Simply being in the community is not enough. Conversion occurs when our friends decide to embrace God's kingdom story as their own so that they become part of the story line.

10. We need to journey with our friends in the *lifelong process* of allowing the Holy Spirit to conform us to the image of Jesus.

So What?

1. When you study "witnessing" in Acts, you will see that the early Christians had a message with content—Jesus is the Messiah, he fulfilled the Scriptures, he was crucified and buried, he has been raised from the dead, and people need to repent and believe the good news. Their witnessing went far beyond a personal testimony of "what God was doing in their lives." In your view, how does witnessing today compare with the witnessing of the early church?

A Different People

Christians are distinguished from other men neither by country nor language nor the customs they observe. For they neither inhabit cities of their own, nor employ a peculiar form of speech, nor lead a life which is marked out by any singularity. . . . But inhabiting Greek as well as barbarian cities . . . and following the customs of the natives in respect of clothing, food, and the rest of their ordinary conduct, they display to us their wonderful and confessedly paradoxical manner of life. They dwell in fatherlands of their own country, but only as aliens. As citizens they share in all things with others, and yet endure all things as foreigners. . . . They marry as do all; they beget children, but they do not destroy their offspring. They have a common table, but not a common bed. They are in the flesh but they do not live after the flesh. They pass their days on earth, but they are citizens of heaven. They obey the prescribed laws, and at the same time surpass the laws by their lives. They love all men, and are persecuted by all.

—from the early second-century
Epistle to Diognetus,
quoted in Michael Green,
Evangelism in the Early Church, 192

Cross-References

Mark 13:11; Luke 12:8–9; John 4:1–42; 17:15–19; Acts 4:18–20; 8:26–40; Rom. 1:16; 10:9–10; 1 Cor. 2:1–5; 9:19–27; 1 Thess. 1:5; 2 Tim. 1:7–8; 1 Peter 3:15

For Deeper Study

Green, Michael. *Evangelism in the Early Church.* Rev. ed. Grand Rapids: Eerdmans, 2003.

Kallenberg, Brad. *Live to Tell: Evangelism to a Postmodern Age.* Grand Rapids: Brazos Press, 2002.

Long, Jimmy. *Emerging Hope: Strategy for Reaching Postmodern Generations.* 2nd ed. Downers Grove, IL: InterVarsity Press, 2004.

Newman, Randy. *Questioning Evangelism: Engaging People's Hearts the Way Jesus Did.* Grand Rapids: Kregel, 2004.

Tabb, Mark. *Mission to Oz: Reaching Postmoderns Without Losing Your Way.* Chicago: Moody, 2004.

2. Some would say that we spend too much time talking about strategies and methods when we should be focusing on imitating the conviction, passion, and determination of the early church. How would you respond to that sentiment?

3. As you look at the ten-step engagement strategy outlined in Behaving 2, what are your two strongest areas? In what two areas do you want to grow?

4. Michael Green suggests that one of the great needs of the church today is for "those who evangelize to improve their theological understanding, and for those who are theologically competent to come out of their ivory tower and evangelize" (*Evangelism in the Early Church*, 19). What are your ideas for achieving this integration of head, heart, and hands?

5. What is one thing your Christian community could do differently to become more faithful in living out the Great Commission?

Who Cares?

Compassion

Our mission is to go and make disciples of all nations. To fulfill this mission we must get out of our comfortable "Christian" cocoons and subcultures and touch a world full of people looking for life apart from God. As we engage non-Christians in open, honest conversations, we start to see their deep need for a relationship with the one true source of life, Jesus Christ. When we hear their stories, we see them less as a target for soul-winning and more as a person created in God's image who needs to experience life and hope. Instead of condemning or avoiding or manipulating, we begin to feel compassion and sympathy. Our hearts go out to them, and we are led by the Spirit to give our time, possessions, and abilities to draw our friends into a relationship with our Lord. In Becoming 2 we will see that a heart of compassion is more valuable than pious credentials or legalistic purity.

Notice how Jesus' compassion caused him to heal, feed, touch, cleanse, teach, exorcise demons, raise the dead, and forgive the rebellious. The italicized words in these verses all represent the same Greek word:

When Jesus . . . saw a large crowd, he had *compassion* on them and healed their sick. (Matt. 14:14)

Jesus . . . said, "I have *compassion* for these people; they have already been with me three days and have nothing to eat. I do not want to send them away hungry, or they may collapse on the way." (Matt. 15:32)

Jesus had *compassion* on them [two blind men] and touched their eyes. Immediately they received their sight and followed him. (Matt. 20:34)

Filled with *compassion*, Jesus reached out his hand and touched the man. "I am willing," he said. "Be clean!" Immediately the leprosy left him and he was cured. (Mark 1:41–42).

"You have answered correctly . . . Do this and you will live"—In Luke 10:28 Jesus tells the expert in religious law that he had answered the question correctly or accurately (*orthōs*, from which we get our word *orthodox*). But Jesus doesn't stop with "That's the right answer." He adds, "Do this and you will live." Then Jesus tells the parable with its surprise ending—a Samaritan rather than a Jew acts as the neighbor (the hero). Jesus again tells the expert in religious law to "go and do likewise" (cf. the original question in 10:25). Compassion means more than giving the right answer in a theological discussion; it is love demonstrated in sacrificial action.

"took pity"—Here we have a window into the Samaritan's heart. This word "pity" speaks of mercy, sympathy, or tenderhearted compassion. The same word is used in the parable of the prodigal son, where the Father has compassion on his rebellious son (see Luke 15:20). Showing pity, or compassion, causes us to give our time, possessions, abilities, and influence to help a person in need. Instead of "passing by" because of fear or pride, the Samaritan uses his own clothes, oil, wine, donkey, money, and time to take care of the Jewish victim. That's compassion!

When Jesus landed and saw a large crowd, he had *compassion* on them, because they were like sheep without a shepherd. So he began teaching them many things. (Mark 6:34)

It has often thrown him [a demon-possessed boy] into fire or water to kill him. But if you can do anything, *take pity* on us and help us. (Mark 9:22)

When the Lord saw her [a grieving widow], his *heart went out* to her and he said, "Don't cry." (Luke 7:13)

But while he was still a long way off, his father saw him and was filled with *compassion* for him; he ran to his son. (Luke 15:20)

John Stott helps us see what was going on with Jesus:

The eyes of Jesus never missed the sight of need. Nobody could accuse him of being like the priest and the Levite [in the parable of the good Samaritan]. . . . Of both it is written, "he saw him." Yet each saw him without seeing, for he looked the other way, and so "passed by on the other side." Jesus, on the other hand, truly "saw." He was not afraid to look human need in the face, in all its ugly reality. And what he saw invariably moved him to compassion, and so to . . . service. . . . He saw, he felt, he acted. The movement was from the eye to the heart, and from the heart to the hand. His compassion was always aroused by the sight of need, and it always led to constructive action. (*Authentic Christianity*, 37)

A Closer Look—Luke 10:30–37

Find Luke 10 in your Bible. Read about Jesus' encounter with an expert in religious law in 10:25–29. Jesus answers this man's question with a parable—a story that teaches at least one spiritual lesson. Jesus' story is known as the parable of the good Samaritan.

1. Read Luke 10:30–37 carefully and answer the story questions below.

WHO?	WHAT?

WHEN?	WHERE?

WHY?	HOW?

2. Consult a Bible handbook, dictionary, or background commentary to find out more about the following elements of the story. Make a few notes summarizing what you have found.

- Jerusalem to Jericho

- A priest and a Levite

- A Samaritan

Why do you think the expert in religious law said "the one" in verse 37 rather than "the Samaritan"?

Role Reversal

There is a striking reversal of roles here. The Jewish "expert" would have thought of the Jewish victim as a good person and the Samaritan as an evil one. To a Jew there was no such person as a "good" Samaritan. Jesus could have told the story with a Samaritan victim and a Jewish helper, but the role reversal drives the story home by shaking the hearer loose from his preconceptions.

—Walter Liefeld, "Luke," 943–44

Create a scenario that we might experience today that illustrates the same truths as Jesus' parable. Don't worry about writing a full-blown story; just think of a parallel situation.

Crossing the Bridge

What biblical principles do you see in Luke 10:30–37?

-
-
-
-

So What?

1. How has God spoken to you through the parable of the good Samaritan?

2. What kinds of things cause us to "pass by on the other side"?

3. What motivates you to show compassion?

4. Read "Role Reversal" in the sidebar and create your own scenario to illustrate what compassion might look like in our contemporary setting.

5. How do you think God wants us to relate sharing the good news of Jesus Christ (evangelism) with meeting people's physical and social needs (social ministry)? How would you rate your own grasp of this important relationship?

6. As a result of this section on mission, engaging the world, and compassion, what small steps does God want you to take to carry out his mission in this world? How can you help others with the task?

Cross-References
1 Sam. 15:22; Isa. 58:6–7; Mic. 6:8; Matt. 9:9–13; Eph. 4:32; James 2:14–26; 1 Peter 3:8; 1 John 3:17–18

For Deeper Study
Blomberg, Craig L. *Interpreting the Parables.* Downers Grove, IL: InterVarsity Press, 1990.
Bock, Darrell. *Luke.* NIV Application Commentary. Grand Rapids: Zondervan, 1996.
Sider, Ronald J. *Good News and Good Works.* Grand Rapids: Baker, 1993.
Wenham, David. *The Parables of Jesus.* Downers Grove, IL: InterVarsity Press, 1989.

The Grand Finale

The End

The kingdom story began with God creating humans to experience life and enjoy his presence forever. Although Satan and sin did a lot of damage in their bid to destroy the whole project, God's love would not let us go. He sent Jesus Christ to rescue us from the powers of darkness and restore our relationship with him. When we enter into this new relationship, we also become members of God's new community, the church. The Holy Spirit takes up residence within us and begins the process of making us more like Jesus Christ. To fully understand the kingdom story, we need to know how it ends, and that is the subject of Believing 3. (The technical term for the study of final or last things is *eschatology*.)

The story's final chapter is closely tied to Jesus' teaching about the kingdom of God. The kingdom of God is the rule or reign of God. When Jesus began to minister publicly, his main message was "The kingdom of God is near. Repent and believe the good news!" (Mark 1:15; see also Matt. 4:17, 23; Luke 4:42–44). Jesus healed the sick, cast out demons, fed the hungry, and forgave sinners—all signs that the kingdom had arrived. In Jesus, the kingdom of God became a *present reality* (Matt. 11:11–12; 12:28; 18:1–5; Luke 17:20–21). Because his first followers expected him to establish the kingdom fully and totally during their lifetimes, they were crushed when Jesus was crucified. Yet after his resurrection and ascension to heaven, the disciples began to see God's greater plan (see the chart below).

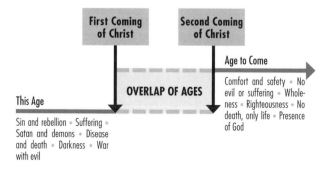

First Coming of Christ

Second Coming of Christ

Age to Come

OVERLAP OF AGES

This Age

Sin and rebellion • Suffering • Satan and demons • Disease and death • Darkness • War with evil

Comfort and safety • No evil or suffering • Wholeness • Righteousness • No death, only life • Presence of God

At Jesus' first coming, the kingdom of God broke into this world. A world filled with sin, rebellion, Satan, darkness, and evil encountered a touch of peace, righteousness, life, and God. When we begin to follow Christ the King, we start to experience "age-to-come" (eternal) life right now. We come alive and get a taste of heaven while still living on earth. The apostle Paul says that we have been "rescued . . . from the dominion of darkness and brought . . . into the kingdom of the Son" (Col. 1:13). We are new people living in an old world. God has started his kingdom project, but he has not completely finished it. The kingdom of God has *already* arrived, but it has *not yet* come in all its fullness. The grand project has been launched, but it has not been finished. The kingdom of God also has a *future dimension* (Matt. 6:10; 25:34; 26:29; Luke 19:11–27). We are living in enemy-occupied territory between God's initial invasion (Jesus' first coming) and his total defeat of evil (Jesus' second coming). We are living in the overlap between this age and the age to come. Our circumstance explains a lot:

- We experience God's forgiveness, but we still sin and will never be perfect in this life.
- We have victory over death, but we will one day die physically.
- We still get sick, and not all Christians will experience healing.
- We live in the Spirit, but Satan will continue to attack and may do damage.
- God lives within us, but we do not yet live in God's presence.

Because of the "already/not fully" reality of the kingdom of God, we will experience victories as well as struggles until Jesus returns—an event that Christians throughout history have longed for. The return of Christ lies at the heart of our focal passage from 1 Thessalonians.

A Closer Look—1 Thessalonians 4:13–18

In this section of his letter, Paul is responding to his readers' confusion about the return of Christ and the events associated with it, especially the resurrection from the dead. In the blank space alongside the passage, *outline Paul's train of thought* as he seeks to give these believers hope by answering their questions.

"God will bring with Jesus"—The fact that Jesus died and rose again serves as a guarantee that God will bring to life those who have fallen asleep in him. Rather than suggesting that people will come down from heaven with Jesus, this expression refers to God's people being raised from the dead and gathered to Jesus when he returns.

"fallen asleep"—This expression was a popular metaphor for physical death in the first-century world, used by pagans and Christians alike (see John 11:11–14; 1 Cor. 15:20). Because Jesus has been raised, death no longer robs us of hope. We certainly grieve the death of believers, but we do not despair since God promises to raise them from the dead also.

"caught up"—This word, meaning "to snatch or seize," occurs fourteen times in the New Testament. Only here in 1 Thessalonians 4:17 does it refer to the catching up, or rapture, of believers. This passage teaches us that the Rapture occurs at the second coming of Christ, that it will be accompanied by loud, visible, public acts of God, and that it will serve to unite all believers ("awake" or "asleep") to the Lord forever.

SCRIPTURE NOTES

¹³Brothers and sisters, we do not want you to be uninformed about those who sleep in death, so that you do not grieve like the rest, who have no hope. ¹⁴We believe that Jesus died and rose again, and so we believe that God will bring with

Jesus those who have fallen asleep in him. [15]According to the Lord's word, we tell you that we who are still alive, who are left till the coming of the Lord, will certainly not precede those who have fallen asleep. [16]For the Lord himself will come down from heaven, with a loud command, with the voice of the archangel and with the trumpet call of God, and the dead in Christ will rise first. [17]After that, we who are still alive and are left will be caught up together with them in the clouds to meet the Lord in the air. And so we will be with the Lord forever. [18]Therefore encourage one another with these words. (TNIV)

When the Play Ends

Why is God landing in this enemy-occupied world in disguise and starting a sort of secret society to undermine the devil? Why is He not landing in force, invading it? Is it that He is not strong enough? Well, Christians think He is going to land in force; we do not know when. But we can guess why He is delaying. He wants to give us the chance of joining His side freely. I do not suppose you and I would have thought much of a Frenchman who waited till the Allies were marching into Germany and then announced he was on our side. God will invade. But I wonder whether people who ask God to interfere so openly and directly in our

(continued on the next page)

Crossing the Bridge

What theological principles do you see in 1 Thessalonians 4:13–18?

-

-

-

Important Parts in the Story's Last Chapter

The end of God's kingdom story includes many important topics. Here are the main ones.

Death

One thing is certain in life—we will all die (Rom. 5:12; 6:23). The time of our death is beyond our control (Eccl. 8:8; James 4:14). Although death is described as the last enemy (1 Cor. 15:26), Christ has conquered death, and those who follow Christ don't have to fear death (Ps. 23:4; Phil. 1:21). When Christ returns, he will kill death (1 Cor. 15:54–56).

The Second Coming of Jesus

Whereas his first coming was humble, Jesus' second coming will be a public, visible, spectacular event (Matt. 24:30–31; Heb. 9:28). His coming will be sudden—like a thief in the night (Matt. 24:44; 1 Thess. 5:1–3)—and only the Father knows the time (Matt. 24:36). Jesus will return to gather his people, judge the wicked, and establish his kingdom in all its fullness (Matt. 25:31–32; Rev. 19:11–16).

The Resurrection of the Dead

All people will be raised from the dead (John 5:23–29). Believers will be raised to eternal life (John 6:40), while unbelievers will be raised in order to be condemned (Matt. 25:46; John 5:29). Christians will be given resurrection bodies (1 Cor. 15), created for perfect life in the new heaven and new earth.

The Last Judgment

All people will face judgment after death (2 Tim. 4:1; Heb. 9:27). Christians will not be condemned for their sin (John 5:24; Rom. 8:1–2), but we must give an account for how we lived our lives (Rom. 14:12; 1 Cor. 3:12–15; 2 Cor. 5:10). Our Judge will also be our Savior (John 5:22; Acts 10:42). Unbelievers will be condemned because they have not trusted in Christ (John 12:48; 2 Peter 3:7; Jude 15; Rev. 20:15).

Hell or Heaven

Hell is a real place of punishment for those who reject Jesus (Matt. 13:39–43; 25:41; Rev. 20:15). People in hell experience the darkness of eternal separation from God (Matt. 25:46; 2 Thess. 1:9). In contrast, heaven is the eternal home of God's people. In the new heaven and new earth, we will live an embodied life (1 Cor. 15:35–37), a community life (Rev. 21:1–3), a pain-free, sin-free, death-free life (Rev. 21:4), a worshipful life (Rev. 21:22), a life of meaningful work (Rev. 22:3, 5), a diverse life (Rev. 22:2), and a God-centered life (Rev. 22:4). What God originally planned for the garden of Eden will finally come to pass in the heavenly garden, all because of the battle won in the garden of Gethsemane.

So What?

1. Some of us are "already" Christians (naive optimists who expect perfection now), while others are "not fully" Christians (gloomy pessimists overwhelmed by human problems). Which one are you most like? How can you become more of an "already/not fully" Christian, a biblical realist who admits struggles *and* celebrates victories?

world quite realise what it will be like when He does. When that happens, it is the end of the world. When the author walks on to the stage the play is over. God is going to invade, all right: but what is the good of saying you are on His side then, when you see the whole natural universe melting away like a dream and something else—something it never entered your head to conceive—comes crashing in; something so beautiful to some of us and so terrible to others that none of us will have any choice left? For this time it will be God without disguise; something so overwhelming that it will strike either irresistible love or irresistible horror into every creature. It will be too late then to choose your side. There is no use saying you choose to lie down when it has become impossible to stand up. That will not be the time for choosing: it will be the time when we discover which side we really have chosen, whether we realised it before or not. Now, today, this moment is our chance to choose the right side. God is holding back to give us that chance. It will not last forever. We must take it or leave it.

—C. S. Lewis,
Mere Christianity, 64–65

Cross-References

Matt. 24–25; Mark 13; 1 Cor. 15:12–58; 1 Thess. 5:1–11; 2 Peter 3:3–14; Rev. 19–22

For Deeper Study

Beale, G. K. *1–2 Thessalonians.* IVP New Testament Commentary. Downers Grove, IL: InterVarsity Press, 2003.

Hays, J. Daniel, J. Scott Duvall, and C. Marvin Pate. *Dictionary of Biblical Prophecy and End Times.* Grand Rapids: Zondervan, 2007.

Holmes, Michael W. *1 and 2 Thessalonians.* NIV Application Commentary. Grand Rapids: Zondervan, 1998.

2. Think about the theological principles you listed under "Crossing the Bridge." What is the main message you see in 1 Thessalonians 4:13–18?

3. Do you think all the talk about things like the tribulation, the rapture, the Antichrist, Armageddon, and the millennium prevents us from seeing the main message about how the story ends? Explain your thinking.

4. Does the ending of God's kingdom story surprise you in any way? Would you have planned things differently? Why?

5. Do you think knowing more about how the story ends will affect your life in any way right now?

6. In light of how the story ends, what should be the focus of our Christian community?

The Wilderness

Persevering

The Bible closes with Jesus' words, "I am coming soon," followed by the response, "Come, Lord Jesus." (Rev. 22:20). The next line, the very last line in the entire Bible, reads, "The grace of the Lord Jesus be with God's people. Amen" (v. 21). That makes sense. Christians who are dealing with tough times actually long for Christ's return. His coming will mean an end to pain, sickness, injustice, sin, Satan, and death. But while we await his return, we need grace to remain faithful and stay the course. As John Ortberg reminds us, "God takes his people to the Promised Land by way of the desert. He is the God of the roundabout way" (*Love Beyond Reason*, 83). The wilderness is not a fun place, but it can be a formative place as we learn to trust God at a deeper level. Behaving 3 is about the need to obey God, not only when we feel his presence, but also when he seems silent and distant. We are called to endure a long-distance race, not a sprint.

When I was in college, I ran the Dallas White Rock marathon. In case you're not into running, a marathon is a little over twenty-six miles. My friend Kenny Burt and I trained for four months. Sometimes those late afternoon runs of six, eight, or twelve miles were fun, and we felt like we could run forever. At other times, even a four-mile run would drain us and leave us discouraged and doubting. Neither of us had ever run twenty-six miles, and we weren't sure if we could actually do it. But we kept training, whether we felt like it or not. Day after day, we pounded the pavement. We endured heat, rude drivers, leg cramps, wind, cold, darkness, rain, exhaustion, and thirst in order to run the Rock in December. The big day arrived and, loaded with carbohydrates, we began the race. I've never felt a surge of adrenaline like I felt during those first few miles. We settled into a pace for the next ten to fifteen miles. Then around mile eighteen or so, we entered

"cloud of witnesses"—The great "cloud" refers to the heroes of faith mentioned in Hebrews 11. How are they witnesses? While it's possible that they are spectators watching our every move, it's more likely that they bear witness to God's faithfulness. They persevered and found God faithful. Rather than the heroes watching us, we are looking to them for encouragement that perseverance is worth the price.

"everything that hinders"—This refers to a weight, burden, or hindrance. In the ancient world runners would shed any excess weight in order to move freely and run faster (some ran naked). Sin certainly entangles us, as the next part of the sentence makes clear, but some things that are not sinful in themselves may weigh us down. We should get rid of anything that hinders our passionate devotion to Christ.

"run with perseverance"—This figure of speech reminds us that the Christian life requires action and effort. God expects us to "run." Also, the race we run is more like a marathon and less like a short sprint. To run with perseverance means to persist and stick with it over a lifetime, through easy times as well as hard times.

"race marked out"—This phrase means to "lie before." As runners see the course marked out before them, so Christians see the path of endurance laid out for us. We see where we must go, but actually running the race is the hard part.

new territory. We got separated and were running alone. I experienced severe leg cramps. The wind was very strong that day, and, like it or not, I had to stop and stretch many times. Both of us hit "the wall"—a common experience for marathoners around mile twenty, where your body completely runs out of gas. I kept on putting one foot in front of the other, not knowing for sure if mile twenty-six would ever arrive. Through pain, strong winds, utter fatigue, and a constant urge to quit, I persevered to the end. We both finished the race. We never talked much about who "won" since we both came to understand winning as just finishing the grueling twenty-six-mile race. It was an unforgettable experience.

The Bible speaks of life as an endurance race in Hebrews 12:1–2. Take a moment and read Hebrews 11. What is your first reaction to those who endured the race of faith?

Perseverance is a prominent theme in the New Testament. Below you will find a few key places where perseverance is mentioned (the actual translation is given in parentheses). Read each passage and its surrounding context, and write a short statement in the space provided, explaining how perseverance is significant in this setting.

- Matthew 24:13 ("stands firm")

- Luke 8:15 ("persevering")

- Romans 2:7 ("persistence")

- Romans 5:3–4 ("perseverance")

- 2 Corinthians 1:6 ("patient endurance")

- Colossians 1:10–12 ("endurance")

- 1 Thessalonians 1:3 ("endurance")

- 2 Thessalonians 1:4 ("perseverance")

- 2 Thessalonians 3:5 ("perseverance")

- Hebrews 10:36 ("persevere")

- James 1:2–4 ("perseverance")

- James 1:12 ("perseveres")

- James 5:11 ("persevered")

A Closer Look—Hebrews 12:1–2

As you look closely at our focal passage, notice conjunctions, reasons, figures of speech, commands, descriptions, lists, contrasts, important words, and so on. Also note that this text has one main command (in bold) surrounded by three supporting statements.

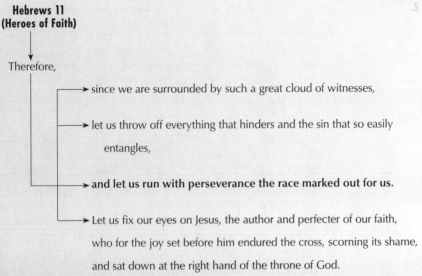

**Hebrews 11
(Heroes of Faith)**

Therefore,

→ since we are surrounded by such a great cloud of witnesses,

→ let us throw off everything that hinders and the sin that so easily entangles,

→ **and let us run with perseverance the race marked out for us.**

→ Let us fix our eyes on Jesus, the author and perfecter of our faith, who for the joy set before him endured the cross, scorning its shame, and sat down at the right hand of the throne of God.

Crossing the Bridge

What theological principles do you see in Hebrews 12:1–2?

-

-

-

At some point every Christian walks through the wilderness. John of the Cross, who endured persecution and imprisonment for his faith, referred to this spiritual desert as the "dark night of the soul"—a time when we don't feel God's presence, when God doesn't seem to answer prayer or speak

Why Valleys?

Remember, in the Screwtape Letters *everything is reversed as an older demon gives advice to a younger demon about how to tempt humans.*

Now it may surprise you to learn that in His [God's] efforts to get permanent possession of a soul, He relies on troughs [valleys] even more than peaks; some of His special favourites have gone through longer and deeper troughs than anyone else. . . . He really does want to fill the universe with a lot of loathsome little replicas of Himself—creatures whose life, on its miniature scale, will be qualitatively like His own, not because He has absorbed them but because their wills freely conform to His. We [Satan and his demons] want cattle who finally become food; He wants servants who can finally become sons. . . . And that is where the troughs come in. . . . Merely to override a human will (as His felt presence in any but the faintest and most mitigated degree would certainly do) would be for Him useless. He cannot ravish. He can only woo. . . . He is prepared to do a little overriding at the beginning. . . . Sooner or later He withdraws, if not in fact, at least from their conscious experience, all those supports and incentives. He leaves the creatures to stand up on their own legs—to carry out from the will alone duties which have lost all relish. It is during such trough periods, much more

(continued on the next page)

through his Word, when worship is dull and temptation grows stronger. We lack passion and direction, and God seems far away. In a word, we feel forsaken. We confess our sin, we plead with God for guidance, and nothing seems to bring back the good old days of sweet communion with our Lord. Richard Foster refers to this experience as "God's purifying silence."

> Through all of this, paradoxically, God is purifying our faith by threatening to destroy it. We are led to a profound and holy distrust of all superficial drives and human strivings. We know more deeply than ever before our capacity for infinite self-deception. Slowly we are being taken off of vain securities and false allegiances. Our trust in all exterior and interior results is being shattered so that we can learn faith in God alone. Through our barrenness of soul God is producing detachment, humility, patience, perseverance. (*Prayer*, 22)

In a chapter titled "When God Seems Distant," Rick Warren offers helpful advice about what to do when you don't feel God's presence (*Purpose-Driven Life*, 110–13):

1. *Tell God exactly how you feel.* Pour out your heart to God (Job 7:11; 29:4). Unloading your feelings on God through prayer can actually be a confession of faith (see "Prayer Paralysis?" on page 27). Pray the lament Psalms as ways of speaking honestly with God (see Pss. 3–8, 10, 12–13, 15–17, 21–22, 25–26, 28, 31, 35, 38, 42–44, 51, 54–61, 69–71, 74, 79–80, 83, 86, 88, 90, 94, 102, 109, 120, 130–132, 139–141, 143).
2. *Think back to what God has already done for you.* You can trust God for the future because you can trace his faithfulness to you in the past. Reflect on how much God has already done for you by sending Jesus to die on the cross. Then turn to your own life and consider how God has been faithful to you personally.
3. *Focus on God's unchanging character.* God's nature does not change even when our circumstances do. Remind yourself that God is good and loving, great and powerful, that he has a plan for your life and that he is in control.
4. *Trust God to keep his promises.* God's word is more reliable than our emotions. Trust that God is doing a work in your life although you simply don't understand it at the moment.

So What?

1. Right now in your life, what does it involve for you to persevere or endure?

2. In our focal passage there is one main command surrounded by three supporting statements. If we neglect these supports, it will be more difficult to carry out the main command to run with perseverance. Evaluate how you are doing in the supporting areas.

   a. How can you find encouragement from those who have already persevered? Do you read the Scriptures consistently? Do you read biographies of influential Christians of the past?

   b. Sin certainly causes us to stumble, but are there also permissible things in your life that might not be profitable? What is hindering your ability to persevere?

   c. How Jesus-focused are you? It's easy to focus on good things, even religious things, and lose focus on Jesus Christ. When is the last time you read the Gospels?

3. Have you ever been through a "dark night" or "trough"? How did God change you through this experience? What dangers to our faith does the dark night bring?

4. What role should our feelings play in our relationship with God?

5. In addition to the advice given by Rick Warren earlier, what helps you to persevere in the wilderness?

than during the peak periods, that it is growing into the sort of creature He wants it to be. Hence the prayers offered in the state of dryness are those which please Him best. . . . He cannot "tempt" to virtue as we do to vice. He wants them to learn to walk and must therefore take away His hand; and if only the will to walk is there He is pleased even with their stumbles. . . . Our [Satan's] cause is never more in danger than when a human, no longer desiring, but still intending, to do our Enemy's [God's] will, looks round upon a universe from which every trace of Him seems to have vanished, and asks why he has been forsaken, and still obeys.

—C. S. Lewis,
Screwtape Letters, 38–40

Cross-References
See the Scripture references on pages 54–55 with regard to perseverance.

For Deeper Study
Carson, D. A. *How Long, O, Lord? Reflections on Suffering and Evil*. Grand Rapids: Baker, 1990.

Guthrie, George H. *Hebrews*. NIV Application Commentary. Grand Rapids: Zondervan, 1998.

Lewis, C. S. *The Problem of Pain*. New York: Macmillan, 1962.

Yancey, Philip. *Reaching for the Invisible God*. Grand Rapids: Zondervan, 2000.

Yancey, Philip. *Where Is God When It Hurts?* Anniversary edition. Grand Rapids: Zondervan, 2002.

BECOMING 3 ■■■■■

Are We There Yet?

Hope

Do you ever feel like a kid riding in the back seat of a car, asking God that old, familiar question, "Are we there yet?" or "How much farther?" That is actually a very biblical question, asked by many faithful followers (cf. Pss. 6:3; 13:1; 35:17; 89:46; Hab. 1:2; Rev. 6:10). The good news is that the story does have an ending. The bad news is that we aren't there yet. As Craig Barnes says, "Christians will always live carrying in one hand the promises of how it will be and in the other hand the reality of how it is" (*Yearning*, 16). God is taking us somewhere. There is a real destination, but we haven't arrived. We're still on the journey. As a result, we are called to persevere. In order to survive this time between the "already" and the "not fully," we need hope; Becoming 3 is about biblical hope.

In our culture, the word *hope* is almost as confusing as the word *love*. We can say "I hope it doesn't rain at our reception," or "I hope the Dallas Cowboys make the playoffs," or "I put my hope in Christ." To understand what the Bible means by hope, we first need to know what it does not mean. In the Bible hope is not the same thing as wishing for something, as in wishing against rain or for the Cowboys. When you wish for something, you have no assurance that it will happen and no basis for "hoping" one way or the other. Our wishes have no connection to reality.

Unlike wishful thinking, biblical hope is *based on the character of God*. Nothing is more sure and certain. We know God's character because of what he has done in the past and what he is doing in the present. In the past, God defeated sin and Satan through the death and resurrection of his Son, Jesus Christ. In the present God has given us his very own Spirit, who is his "seal" of ownership and protection as well as a "deposit guaranteeing" our future inheritance (Eph. 1:13–14). Our hope is more than wishing, because our hope rests on God's character. God himself is our hope. Our future is certain.

Biblical hope is a confident reliance on God to stay true to his word and keep his promises. Hope is a disciplined (1 Peter 1:13), sacrificial (1 Cor. 9:24–27), purifying (1 John 3:3), joyful (Rom. 12:12) waiting on the Lord. As the old song says, "This world is not my home. I'm just passing through." We are journeying to a more permanent home, a heavenly home (Heb. 11:10, 16). Hope means living in the present in light of a rock-solid certain future. This future is based on the character of God, and we know who God is because of what he has done and is doing. We will "get there" because our Father always keeps his promises.

Our focal passage is Romans 8:22–25, a text that tells the true story of our present struggles and our hope for the future. Enjoy!

A Closer Look—Romans 8:22–25

Read the focal passage carefully, looking at prepositional phrases, repeated words, time indicators, explanations, purpose statements, contrasts, figures of speech, and so on.

²²We know that the whole creation has been groaning as in the pains of childbirth right up to the present time. ²³Not only so, but we ourselves, who have the firstfruits of the Spirit, groan inwardly as we wait eagerly for our adoption as sons, the redemption of our bodies. ²⁴For in this hope we were saved. But hope that is seen is no hope at all. Who hopes for what he already has? ²⁵But if we hope for what we do not yet have, we wait for it patiently.

1. From the context, why does creation and why do Christians "groan"?

> **Hopelessness Is Hell**
> Living without hope is no longer living. Hell is hopelessness and it is not for nothing that at the entrance to Dante's hell there stand the words: "Abandon hope, all you who enter here."
> —Jürgen Moltmann,
> *Theology of Hope*, 32

"firstfruits of the Spirit"—The Holy Spirit serves as God's promise that he is not finished with us yet. The Spirit is like a down payment or a pledge guaranteeing our future. The Spirit is the unbreakable connection between the beginning and the end of our experience of God's salvation (cf. 2 Cor. 1:22; 5:5; Eph. 1:14). The Spirit joins the "already" to the "not fully" in God's great salvation story.

"redemption of our bodies"—In Romans 8:14–17 we read that Christians have already been adopted as God's children. A few verses later we read that "we wait eagerly for our adoption" (v. 23). So have we already been adopted or not? Yes, when we entered a relationship with Jesus, we were adopted as God's children, but there is more to our adoption—the redemption of [not from] our bodies. What we experience now is real, but there is more to come. Redemption is both past and future. We are God's children now, but one day God will transform our bodies into bodies fit for a new heaven and new earth (see 1 Cor. 15).

"wait for it patiently"—Between the already and the not fully, we hope and wait. The word "patiently" could be translated "with endurance" or "with perseverance." This is the same word that we encountered in Hebrews 12:1–2 (see Behaving 3). We persevere through hardship and suffering, waiting for Christ to return.

2. List all the characteristics of hope you can find in this passage.

Crossing the Bridge

What biblical principles do you see in Romans 8:22–25?

-

-

-

The Beginning and the End

"In the beginning God . . ." so the story begins. We were created to experience perfect community, but Satan and sin entered the picture and brought death. Because of his love, God came to our rescue. Through the life, death, and resurrection of Jesus, the gift of his Holy Spirit, and his new community the church, God is reversing the curse (see chart, pages 60–61). He wants us to experience life and hope. That is his heart, and our opportunity. To God be the glory!

GENESIS 1–11	REVELATION 19–22	
Sinful people scattered	God's people unite to sing his praises	19:6–7
"Marriage" of Adam and Eve	Marriage of Last Adam and his bride, the church	19:7; 21:2, 9
God abandoned by sinful people	God's people (New Jerusalem, bride of Christ) made ready for God; marriage of Lamb	19:7–8; 21:2, 9–21
Exclusion from bounty of Eden	Invitation to marriage supper of Lamb	19:9
Satan introduces sin into world	Satan and sin are judged	19:11–21; 20:7–10
The Serpent deceives humanity	The ancient Serpent is bound "to keep him from deceiving the nations"	20:2–3
God gives humans dominion over the earth	God's people will reign with him forever	20:4, 6; 22:5
People rebel against the true God resulting in physical and spiritual death	God's people risk death to worship the true God and thus experience life	20:4–6
Sinful people sent away from life	God's people have their names written in the Book of Life	20:4–6, 15; 21:6, 27

Death enters the world	Death is put to death	20:14; 21:4
God creates first heaven and earth, eventually cursed by sin	God creates a new heaven and earth where sin is nowhere to be found	21:1
Water symbolizes unordered chaos	There is no longer any sea (symbol of evil)	21:1
Sin brings pain and tears	God comforts his people and removes crying and pain	21:4
Sinful humanity cursed with wandering (exile)	God's people given a permanent home	21:3
Community forfeited	Genuine community experienced	21:3, 7
Sinful people are banished from presence of God	God lives among his people	21:3, 7, 22; 22:4
Creation begins to grow old and die	All things are made new	21:5
Water used to destroy wicked humanity	God quenches thirst with water from spring of life	21:6; 22:1
"In the beginning God . . ."	"I am the Alpha and the Omega, the Beginning and the End."	21:6
Sinful humanity suffers a wandering exile in the land	God gives his children an inheritance	21:7
Sin enters the world	Sin banished from God's city	21:8, 27; 22:15
Sinful humanity separated from presence of holy God	God's people experience God's holiness (cubed city = Holy of Holies)	21:15–21
God creates light and separates it from darkness	No more night or natural light; God himself is the source of light	21:23; 22:5
Languages of sinful humanity confused	God's people is a multicultural people	21:24, 26; 22:2
Sinful people sent away from garden	New heaven/earth includes a garden	22:2
Sinful people forbidden to eat from tree of life	God's people may eat freely from the tree of life	22:2, 14
Sin results in spiritual sickness	God heals the nations	22:2
Sinful people cursed	The curse removed from redeemed humanity and they become a blessing	22:3
Sinful people refuse to serve/obey God	God's people serve him	22:3
Sinful people ashamed in God's presence	God's people will "see his face"	22:4

Chart taken from *The Story of Israel* by J. Daniel Hays, C. Marvin Pate, E. Randolph Richards, W. Dennis Tucker Jr., Preben Vang, and J. Scott Duvall. Copyright © 2004 by J. Daniel Hays, C. Marvin Pate, E. Randolph Richards, W. Dennis Tucker Jr., Preben Vang, and J. Scott Duvall. Used with permission of InterVarsity Press, PO Box 1400, Downers Grove, IL 60515. http://www.ivpress.com/.

Not Just a New Heaven

Then I saw a new heaven and a new earth, for the old heaven and the old earth had disappeared. And the sea was also gone. And I saw the holy city, the new Jerusalem, coming down from God out of heaven like a beautiful bride prepared for her husband. I heard a loud shout from the throne, saying, "Look, the home of God is now among his people! He will live with them, and they will be his people. God himself will be with them. He will remove all of their sorrows, and there will be no more death or sorrow or crying or pain. For the old world and its evils are gone forever." And the one sitting on the throne said, "Look, I am making all things new!" And then he said to me, "Write this down, for what I tell you is trustworthy and true." And he also said, "It is finished! I am the Alpha and the Omega—the Beginning and the End. To all who are thirsty I will give the springs of the water of life without charge! All who are victorious will inherit all these blessings, and I will be their God, and they will be my children.

—Revelation 21:1–7 NLT

For Deeper Study

Dockery, David S. *Our Christian Hope.* Nashville: LifeWay, 1998.

Long, Jimmy. *Emerging Hope: Strategy for Reaching Postmodern Generations.* 2nd ed. Downers Grove, IL: InterVarsity Press, 2004.

Moo, Douglas J. *Romans.* NIV Application Commentary. Grand Rapids: Zondervan, 2000.

So What?

1. What is the difference between wishful thinking and biblical hope?

2. What most excites you about our permanent home?

3. Is the biblical concept of a resurrected body in the new heaven and new earth different from the concept of heaven you have heard about all your life?

4. As you read through the Genesis-Revelation chart above, which lines stand out the most to you? Why?

5. What can you and your community do to help you experience hope at a deeper level?

6. How can your Christian community better communicate hope to a culture that is desperate for hope?

Barnes, M. Craig. *Yearning: Living Between How It Is and How It Ought to Be.* Downers Grove, IL: InterVarsity Press, 1992.

Duvall, J. Scott, and J. Daniel Hays. *Grasping God's Word: A Hands-On Approach to Reading, Interpreting, and Applying the Bible.* 2nd ed. Grand Rapids: Zondervan, 2005.

Foster, Richard J. *Prayer: Finding the Heart's True Home.* San Francisco: HarperSanFrancisco, 1992.

Gray, Alice, ed. *Stories for the Heart: Over 100 Stories to Encourage Your Soul.* Sisters, OR: Multnomah, 1996.

Green, Michael. *Evangelism in the Early Church.* Rev. ed. Grand Rapids: Eerdmans, 2003.

Kallenberg, Brad. *Live to Tell: Evangelism to a Postmodern Age.* Grand Rapids: Brazos Press, 2002.

Laubach, Frank. *Letters by a Modern Mystic.* Westwood, NJ: Revell, 1958.

Lewis, C. S. *The Great Divorce.* New York: Macmillan, 1946.

————. *Letters to Malcolm Chiefly on Prayer.* New York: Harcourt, 1964.

————. *Mere Christianity.* New York: Macmillan, 1952.

————. *The Screwtape Letters.* New York: Macmillan, 1961.

Liefeld, Walter L. "Luke" in *Expositor's Bible Commentary,* vol. 8, ed. Frank E. Gaebelein. Grand Rapids: Zondervan, 1984.

Long, Jimmy. *Emerging Hope: Strategy for Reaching Postmodern Generations.* 2nd ed. Downers Grove, IL: InterVarsity Press, 2004.

Moltmann, Jürgen. *Theology of Hope.* Minneapolis: Fortress, 1993.

Moo, Douglas J. *Romans.* NIV Application Commentary. Grand Rapids: Zondervan, 2000.

Murray, Andrew. *With Christ in the School of Prayer.* Grand Rapids: Revell, 1895.

Nouwen, Henri J. M. *The Only Necessary Thing.* New York: Crossroad, 1999.

Ortberg, John. *Everybody's Normal Till You Get to Know Them.* Grand Rapids: Zondervan, 2003.

————. *The Life You've Always Wanted.* Grand Rapids: Zondervan, 1997.

————. *Love Beyond Reason: Moving God's Love From Your Head to Your Heart.* Grand Rapids: Zondervan, 1998.

Piper, John. *Let the Nations Be Glad: The Supremacy of God in Missions.* 2nd ed. Rev. and exp. Grand Rapids: Baker, 2003.

Sider, Ronald J. *Good News and Good Works.* Grand Rapids: Baker, 1993.

Stott, John R. W. *Authentic Christianity: From the Writings of John Stott.* Ed. Timothy Dudley-Smith. Downers Grove, IL: InterVarsity Press, 1996.

Tabb, Mark. *Mission to Oz: Reaching Postmoderns Without Losing Your Way.* Chicago: Moody, 2004.

Warren, Rick. *The Purpose-Driven Life.* Grand Rapids: Zondervan, 2002.

Wilkins, Michael J. *Matthew.* NIV Application Commentary. Grand Rapids: Zondervan, 2004.

Willard, Dallas. *Renovation of the Heart.* Colorado Springs: NavPress, 2002.

————. *The Spirit of the Disciplines.* San Francisco: HarperSanFrancisco, 1988.

J Scott Duvall is professor of New Testament at Ouachita Baptist University, a Christian liberal-arts college in Arkansas, where he teaches Spiritual Formation, Interpreting the Bible, Greek, and New Testament Studies. He received his B.A. from Ouachita and his M.Div. and Ph.D. from Southwestern Seminary, and has been teaching at OBU since 1989. He also serves as copastor of Fellowship Church of Arkadelphia, Arkansas.

Duvall's other publications include *Grasping God's Word, Journey into God's Word, Preaching God's Word, Biblical Greek Exegesis, The Story of Israel, The Dictionary of Biblical Prophecy and End Times*, and *Experiencing God's Story of Life and Hope: A Workbook for Spiritual Formation*.